PILGRIMAGE OF THE HEART

BENEDICTA WARD

SLG Press
Convent of the Incarnation
Fairacres Oxford OX4 1TB

ISBN 0 7283 0155 5
ISSN 0307-1405

'Pilgrimage of the Heart' was originally given as a lecture at an international and inter-disciplinary Conference on Pilgrimage, held at University College, Cork, in July 2000.

Printed and bound by Will Print, Oxford, England

I TAKE my title from a poem by George Herbert, entitled 'Prayer':

> Prayer the Churches banquet, Angels age
> Gods breath in man returning to his birth,
> The soul in paraphrase, heart in pilgrimage,
> The Christian plummet sounding heav'n and earth ...
> Church-bels beyond the starres heard, the souls bloud,
> The land of spices; something understood.[1]

I suggest that 'the heart in pilgrimage' is the basic meaning of Christian pilgrimages, whatever form they take, and that this inner sense of pilgrimage is also a uniting element in human life. The *Oxford Dictionary of the Christian Church*, however, has no such high-class definition for pilgrimages; they are practical tours, mercenary even: they are defined as 'journeys to holy places undertaken from motives of devotion in order to obtain supernatural help or as acts of penance or thanksgiving.'[2] These were indeed the motives uppermost in the minds of the most famous of all pilgrims in Chaucer's *Canterbury Tales*, and that is the usual picture that comes to mind when the word is mentioned. It is in the spring that pilgrims set out:

> Thanne longen folk to goon on pilgrimages,
> And palmeres for to seken straunge strondes,
> To ferne halwes, kowthe in sondry londes;
> And specially from every shires ende
> In Engelond to Caunterbury they wende,
> The hooly blisful martir for to seke,
> That hem hath holpen whan that they were seeke.[3]

The pilgrimage was a cheerful trip, in good company, with a definite place to go, with personal rewards in mind, for a limited season, with return home at the end of it. But even in Chaucer's day there were more serious challenges to the tourist version of pilgrimage; Langland, for instance, echoed later by Erasmus, took a severe view of 'pilgrims and palmers full of clever talk', and for himself chose another kind of pilgrimage:

> I swear by the Holy Rood of Lucca to devote all that is left of my life to the worship of Truth ... and I will be His pilgrim, following the plough for poor men's sake.[4]

In fact, the idea of pilgrimage in the Christian church has always been more than a temporary outing. It has provided an image of the inner life of Christians from the earliest times, and that inner strand was present still when the external reality of pilgrimage was emphasised as an increasingly popular form of devotion throughout the Middle Ages. The two concepts were not simple alternatives; they overlapped and the several strands within each were constantly interwoven. There are ambiguities to be examined in these external and internal ideas of Christian pilgrimage. The idea of pilgrimage as dispossession for the individual, as going away from earthly life towards heavenly life both in action and in idea, has a special reference to monasticism as a pattern for the Christian in the journey to the new Jerusalem. It remained as an implicit theme through the later practices of pilgrimage towards a shrine, which seemed to concentrate more on the idea of getting something earthly, whether healing or souvenirs or simply credit. The material side of such visits provoked stern rebuke in the sixteenth century when the idea of pilgrimage was given a new direction, more in line perhaps with the Letter to the Hebrews and the inner journey within the heart: '[They] confessed that they were strangers and pilgrims on the earth. For they that say such things declare plainly that they seek a country ... that is, an heavenly [one]'. (Hebrews 11:13, 14 and 16)

Inner and outer pilgrimage are not two clear and distinct concepts; in some ways what was outer for the Middle Ages is inner for us and vice versa. But within the framework of these two ideas it seems to me possible to disentangle at least five layers of meaning in the complex image of pilgrimage. Two of them are concerned with pilgrimage as detachment, as going out 'away from'; two of them are concerned with longing and desire, with going 'towards'; and one is concerned primarily with penance, something imposed rather than chosen. The first two were primarily a part of the inner pilgrimage of the heart by which those undertaking them returned to their homeland of heaven; the other three might be called mercenary pilgrimages, for simple gain of one kind or another. Clearly they overlap but perhaps it will be useful to examine each in itself briefly.

Firstly, pilgrimage 'from'. This sense of detachment from self, from what is familiar, is the root meaning of *peregrination, per-agros:* to go through the fields, as a stranger, a foreigner, an outsider.[5] The pilgrim is the outsider, one who has left his home, an exile who belongs nowhere. This idea of pilgrimage was frequently linked with Abraham going out from his own country, at the call of God: 'By faith Abraham ... went out not knowing whither he went ... for he looked for a city which hath foundations and whose builder and maker is God.' (Hebrews 11:8 and 10) The Gospels and Paul's Epistles are full of the call to all Christians to leave familiar ways and follow Christ. Early Christian monasticism showed this fundamental Christian calling in large poster-size images. Antony the Great, 'before him no-one had sought the utter desert', heard the gospel read and followed it literally:

> he entered the church ... and it so happened that the Gospel was being read and at that moment he heard the page in which the Lord says to the rich man, 'if you will be perfect, go, sell all that you have and give to the poor and come and

follow me'; he left the church, gave away his property and devoted himself to living as a monk.[6]

It was a movement indeed, but detachment from domesticity was the motive, a going away from all that held back the heart from following Christ. This was true of the many others in the first days of the monastic movement; they left their homes absolutely to live in solitude, to undertake another inner pilgrimage. Some of them wandered from place to place, never settling for fear of becoming attached, and all of them were ready to move away if the place impeded their inner pilgrimage. One of them made himself walk round his village at night to test how detached he was from longing for it.[7] Such detachment, even in its extreme manifestations, was not in itself a guarantee of inner progress: for instance, there was a monk who decided to spend his life in the total detachment of running with a pack of antelopes; he enjoyed it so much that one day he said to God, 'Let me do something really hard for your sake'; and God told him to go into a monastery. A week later the monk said, 'O God, let me go back to the antelopes.'[8] The Irish were especially expert at this sense of detachment and journeying: for instance, the three men in a boat without oars who came, says the *Anglo-Saxon Chronicle* for 891, to the court of Alfred, leaving home with no intention of returning, aiming for nowhere, were 'on pilgrimage for the love of God, going they cared not where';[9] they were, as the author of the life of St Guthlac put it, *viatore Christe*, travelling with Christ.[10] The fictional *Voyage of St Brendan* described another setting out in which it was better to travel hopefully than to arrive: 'from time to time the wind filled their sails though they knew not whence it came or whither it was taking them.'[11]

Secondly, this exile from home could lead to a new home, a new stability. The perpetual wanderer, a pilgrim in the first sense, could become the second kind of pilgrim; the exile from home who went out from his own place might then settle down in another place. The inner pilgrimage was continued but in a stable place. There could be conflict between the two ways: there is a story from Egypt of a recluse who lived alone for many years in her cell in Rome; she was visited by Serapion, one of the more bizarre monks of Egypt who was famous for wandering naked everywhere. He expressed, most unwisely, his indignation that she received credit from the townsfolk as a saint because she did nothing: 'Why are you sitting here and doing nothing?' he asked her; and she replied, 'I am not doing nothing; I am on a journey.'[12] The exile from home became a traveller in his desire for God, travelling in stability. Free from self and domesticity, the pilgrim placed himself in the hands of God and that could lead to any number of things. Columba, leaving Ireland, settled on the Isle of Iona (with, it must be admitted, many missionary visits elsewhere) with a new and stable base, but away from Ireland:

> Delightful I think it to be in the bosom of an isle,
> on the peak of a rock,
> that I might often see the calm of the sea,
> that I might see its heavy waves over the glittering ocean,
> as they chant a melody to their Father in their eternal course.
> That I might see its ebb and its flood tide in their flow,
> that this might be my name a secret name
> 'He who turned his back upon Ireland'.[13]

The point is 'freedom from', an ascetic attitude, and of course the pilgrimage is an inner one in stability. This detachment from the narrow shell of self by pilgrimage in body prompted the soul to allow what Augustine called the healing of the eyes of the mind, so that earthly life was also transfigured, and the eagerness for the final journey to heaven became a passion:

I wish O Son of the living God, ancient eternal king,
for a secret hut in the wilderness
that it may be my dwelling ...
a lovely church, decked with linen,
a dwelling for the God of heaven;
then bright candles over the holy white scriptures.[14]

The monastic pilgrimage of going away from self in order to travel towards that death which is life, stressed the inner motive of the heart in leaving all. But a third layer of pilgrimage saw it more in terms of going towards an earthly goal and coming back again. The first two exile-pilgrimages could use as their underlying theme the great verses of the Epistle to the Philippians: '[He] emptied himself ... and became obedient unto death [for us]'. (Phil. 2:7,8) The theology of dispossession, to live in union with God in Christ reconciling the world to himself, the *kenosis* of Christ the ground of salvation, underlies this monastic sense of pilgrimage in the early period of the Middle Ages. But in the eleventh century the emphasis shifted in two ways: both by re-affirming the inner pilgrimage of stability with a renewed interest in self-knowledge, and also by moving towards *sequela Christi*, following in the actual footsteps of the man of Galilee: 'it was not until the twelfth century that the image of journeying became a popular expression of a spiritual quest'.[15] This was not new; since the fourth century Palestine had been the Holy Land, the earthly place to which pilgrims wanted to go. As Jerome said, 'it is better to live for Jerusalem than to journey to Jerusalem',[16] but there is the undoubted fact that he lived near Jerusalem himself and got there by going on the feet not of the heart but of the legs; it was there that he wished to live and discover the pilgrimage of the heart *nudus nudum christum sequi*.[17] He also admired and described the lengthy pilgrimage of his friend and companion the matron Paula to Egypt and to Jerusalem.[18] Pilgrimage could mean actual mobility in the fourth as in the fourteenth century, not simply freeing oneself from familiar surroundings to seek the Kingdom, but going 'away from' in order to go 'towards' a definite holy place on earth. The chief place of such pilgrimages has always been and still is Jerusalem. The great pilgrimages of the crusades were inspired by love of the earthly place where Christ had lived and died. Though St Paul had made it clear that it is the 'Jerusalem [which] is above which is free' (Gal.4:26) that is the aim and goal of the disciple, still the actual earthly location mattered. There are plenty of records of such pilgrimages, both to Palestine and to Egypt, beginning with the Empress Helena and recorded of John Cassian and Germanus, Postumianus the admirer of Martin of Tours, and those enterprising women Paula, Melania and Egeria. But in the eleventh century there was a new passion, a new emotion, a new desire to walk where Jesus of Nazareth had walked, to follow as his disciples had done. The Russian abbot Daniel and his companions who visited the Holy Sepulchre in the eleventh century, came there in order to 'see with our own eyes all the places that Christ our God had visited for our salvation'.[19] Because of this historical presence on that particular piece of earth, the Holy Land was seen in a new light as one of the places where there was assurance of holiness, a chink through which one could be helped to slip more easily into heaven. Jerusalem was not the only such place; Rome, the place of the martyrs, especially of the grave of St Peter, ran it a close second. Where else could anyone find such assurance of help in the last days than there at the tomb of the chief of the apostles, the keeper of the keys of the Kingdom? After about 900, the other place of distant pilgrimage was the tomb of the apostle James at Compostela in Spain. Sometimes these goals of pilgrimage were places of permanent exile—some of the Anglo-Saxon kings went to Rome and stayed there to die. It is worth remembering the hazards of the long journeys and the possibility that whatever one intended one might not in fact return. But mostly pilgrims came back; it was a journey during which you were counted as a monk to some extent, but it would not involve permanent exile.

Fourthly, it was increasingly possible to go on pilgrimage towards a more local place; a place not entirely remote, the tomb of a local saint. These were the pilgrimages which were most carefully recorded and to which historians have turned their attention in the last fifty years or so. Many of the sick who could not go on a longer pilgrimage could go to their local shrine; sometimes when healed there they would then undertake the longer pilgrimage out of devotion. William of Wales, for instance, whose bent back had for two years prevented him from undertaking a pilgrimage to the Holy Land, came to the shrine of St Frideswide in Oxford in the twelfth century: the saint 'appeared to him, ... and covered him with a white bear's skin ... he sensed that he was cured ... after a few days he set out with a healthy body on a journey to the Holy Sepulchre'.[20] The pilgrims visiting their local shrines wanted personal results and especially the sick came or were brought, in this last ditch attempt to obtain a cure. This type of pilgrimage seems to have been the kind most easily deflected from the solemn matter of making oneself empty enough to receive God; it could become a way of going in order to get, with perhaps little effort involved. It also resulted in the business-sense of those living around the shrines being sharpened; they realised their assets with assiduous collecting of offerings. The extreme of this came perhaps with pilgrimages made by the relics of saints themselves, for example the journeys of the hairs of the Virgin from Laôn in the twelfth century, primarily undertaken as a money-making expedition for church building.[21] It is not the carrying about of relics that is remarkable; there are many instances of relics being carried about personally by individuals, and of relics being taken in procession; what is striking here is the openly mercenary motive expressed. The cathedral of St Mary at Laôn was damaged by fire in 1112 and Bishop Bartholomew launched a campaign to raise money to rebuild it. He sent some of his clergy on fund-raising tours, carrying the relics of the church, most notably the relic of the hairs of the Virgin Mary; 'with us we took the feretory of Our Lady ... to receive the offerings of the faithful'. From Pentecost 1112 until 21 September they toured northern France, stopping in various towns so that the relics could be venerated and offerings made; the party returned with considerable funds and next year from Palm Sunday 1113 the relics went on a second pilgrimage to the south of England, which was thought to be particularly prosperous. Hermann, the canon who wrote the account made it clear that it was by no means an easy journey, and he recorded some remarkable adventures, for instance among the Devon men who defended with their fists their right to own King Arthur against these foreigners, and with the slave traders in Bristol who nearly kidnapped the canons. But they returned home in September with a hundred and twenty marks; the pilgrimage of the relics was a financial success, though it is not easy to link it with the deeper concepts of peregrination.

All these four kinds of pilgrimage were voluntary but fifthly there were the penitential pilgrimages, on which sinners could be sent as a penance for sin not by choice but by command. These began to be imposed in the 6th century and existed in Chaucer's day—the Parson says 'whan a man hath synned openly .... than hooly chirche by juggement destreyneth hym for to do open penaunce ... as for to goon peraventure naked in pilgrimages or barefoot.'[22] The thirteenth century made Rome especially the place for absolution after Innocent III instituted indulgences to be gained by pilgrimage to Rome every fiftieth year, the years of jubilee. The three great shrines of Jerusalem, Rome and Compostela were special places which offered absolution; they were the gates of heaven, the assured places of the patronage of the saints for sinners. Notorious sins, especially public crimes of the great, were given public penance. Sometimes the penitent was told to wear chains on his journey; in one horrific instance a murderer was made to wear the corpse of the man he had murdered, having it fastened to his back all the way from Germany to Spain. Probably he was sent to St James because 'it is plain that whoever goes truly penitent to St James and asks for his help with all his heart will certainly have all his sins blotted out.'[23] A notorious sinner would need influential celestial patronage working for forgiveness and so he would be sent to the places most closely associated with the greatest saints, whether a tomb or the place of a vision, or a relic, or just a church. The distant penitential pilgrimage could even be imposed as a permanent way of life for a great crime. When Innocent III was approached with the story of Robert the Cannibal, he was strict indeed. Robert had been captured during a crusade with his wife and child; when released he confessed that as a captive of the Saracens he had been forced to kill, cook and eat his infant daughter; he also obeyed orders to kill his wife, but had finally collapsed when asked to eat her too. The penance imposed by the Pope included as one of its regulations that he should never sleep in the same place for the rest of his life but travel from one shrine to another, a permanent pilgrim.[24] In this case it was the pilgrimage itself that was absolution—which brings it very close to the permanent pilgrimage undertaken by the monk.

These kinds of pilgrimage were not exclusive. Pilgrimage undertaken for devotion could become a penitential pilgrimage which in turn could become the monastic inner pilgrimage in stability. This is illustrated by the story of a German tanner who undertook a pilgrimage of devotion with companions to Compostela c.1100; there are at least eight versions of this popular story, but the version I quote was that told to Anselm of Canterbury by Abbot Hugh in the monastery of Cluny where Giraldus, the man concerned, ended his days as a monk.

> Giraldus made a vow to go on pilgrimage to St James of Compostela, but just before setting out he went to say goodbye to his mistress and his farewell kiss led to consummation of his lust ... the devil suggested to him that he might as well end so sinful a life ... Giraldus then cut off his own genitals and cut his throat with a knife ... Restored to his body by the prayers of St James, St Peter and the Virgin Mary, he completed his pilgrimage as a penance and then became a monk at Cluny. [25]

The story shows the more or less carefree approach of pilgrims at the beginning of a journey, the expectation however that such a journey would involve the monastic virtue of celibacy, and the conversion of the journey into the inner pilgrimage of the monk after an experience of death and judgement and the power of the intercession of the saints. In this case the secular pilgrim became the monastic pilgrim, but more usually, among the dangers and delights of actual pilgrimage, it was easy to lose sight of any deeper concept. The practical matters of inns for lodging and company on the way, for instance, belonged to the secular world not the religious one, and even with such a devout pilgrim as Paula, Jerome had expressed concern about pilgrimage involving her in such matters; he advised Paulinus not to go for just that reason. Mixed in with the accounts of actual pilgrimages, there was always a thread of doubt, of warning, a desire to stress the basic idea of inner pilgrimage. Augustine, in the

City of God, saw the church on earth as made up of aliens, people without residence permits, the church *in via*, in pilgrimage, and recommended not visits to shrines, but a life-long journey of conversion of heart. For him, the inner pilgrimage, the theme of exile, continued into its resolution in heaven where 'we shall rest and we shall see, we shall see and we shall love, we shall love and we shall praise, behold what shall be in the end without ending.'[26] Bede, the most static and stable of men, hardly ever leaving his monastery at Jarrow, endorsed this concept of inner pilgrimage:

> The house of God which King Solomon built in Jerusalem is a symbol of the holy universal church, chosen from its beginning until its end ... daily it is being built up in peace by the grace of the king ... part of it is in pilgrimage here on earth, part has passed from this harsh pilgrimage and already reigns with him in heaven to wait there with him until the last day when all things shall be put under his feet ... This house is still on a journey, in order to come to the land of promise, yet it is being built in that land of promise in the city of Jerusalem; in the present time the church is in exile, in future it will be at home in peace.[27]

Anselm of Canterbury described the inner search for conformity of life to God as an ascent, a continual pilgrimage of life, concluding his *Proslogion* with longing for the end and goal of the journey:

> My God,
> I pray that I may so know you and love you
> that I may rejoice in you.
> And if I may not do so fully in this life
> let me go on steadily
> to the day when I come to that fullness.[28]

Bernard of Clairvaux, writing to Alexander of Lincoln about a canon who had gone on the pilgrimage called crusade, was even more explicit about the true place of the pilgrim when he says that this Philip has

> entered the holy city and has chosen his heritage ... he is no longer an inquisitive onlooker but a devout inhabitant and an enrolled citizen of Jerusalem ... If you want to know this Jerusalem is Clairvaux. She is the Jerusalem united to the one in heaven by wholehearted devotion, by conformity of life, and by a certain spiritual affinity.[29]

But these monastic writers did not scorn actual pilgrimages: with their concentration on inner pilgrimage, there was a right place for actual pilgrimage; everyone has different needs at different times, sometimes the inner journey would be helped by an outward one. The images of pilgrimage needed external manifestation at some point or the metaphor would not have any meaning, just as at some point there must be actual lovers or the images of the *Song of Songs* relating the soul to God have no inner meaning. So Augustine, Bede, Anselm and Bernard all recommended actual pilgrimage, though always within the overriding purpose of the inner journey. In the twenty-second book of the *City of God*, Augustine expressed delight that Christians should come to visit the shrine of St Stephen in Hippo. In his *Ecclesiastical History* Bede praised the Anglo-Saxon pilgrims to Rome; Anselm listened with interest to stories of pilgrimages, and Bernard sent more men to Jerusalem as crusader-pilgrims than perhaps any other preacher at any time.

The connection is not a simple one of a practical earthly journey contrasted with an inner spiritual journey. The overlap of actual pilgrimage and inner pilgrimage has four possibilities:

1. It was possible to stay and to stay, in other words to be completely lazy and attempt nothing, go nowhere, stay shut within the walls of self, to ignore pilgrimage altogether.

2. It was possible to stay and yet to go, by undertaking the pilgrimage of the heart while remaining in one place, which was the fundamental monastic way.

3. It was possible to go inwardly by longing and desire in the heart and to confirm this by outward pilgrimage with the feet, to be a true pilgrim.

4. It was possible to go on pilgrimage with feet but not with heart, as a tourist, a runaway, or a drop-out from responsibility, a curious inquirer, in which case there had been no real inner movement; the traveller had taken the shell of self with him and whatever its name it was not in essence a pilgrimage at all.

It was the last of these, the mercenary pilgrimage, which attracted criticism from all sides in the sixteenth century. It is necessary here to refer to the fact that pilgrimage was linked to the veneration of saints, to the sense that those on earth were surrounded by a great cloud of witnesses, who could be reached, appealed to, who were alive and accessible, if unpredictable. Bede described this as the sixth age of life now in progress between the first and second coming of Christ, with the seventh age of the saints who are alive in Christ running parallel to the sixth age, both converging on the eighth age, the day of the Lord. Those in the seventh age could be reached and would aid those in the sixth *in hac lacrymarum valle*, and therefore to visit the places associated with them seemed right and natural. But the reformers were critical of anything to do with the cult of saints; the sense of the household of heaven, of a great cloud of witnesses, always near, always accessible, which was the setting for medieval pilgrimage, was seen as an impediment to true knowledge of God and sternly rejected in favour of a simple, personal access to the Lord alone. Most obviously, veneration of and appeal to the saints, led to pilgrimage to shrines in expectation of miracles and a desire for relics, and this could be seen to engender a greed for what Bonhoeffer called 'cheap grace'. The criticisms of the Catholic Erasmus were as searing as those of the Protestant Calvin. Physical pilgrimage was derided and then rejected. Yet it is in the ensuing centuries in the Protestant world that the ideal of inner pilgrimage flowered; not for nothing did I take my title from a seventeenth century Anglican poet. The outward trappings of pilgrimage were given a totally inner meaning as terms used to describe the life of any ordinary Christian. The severe reaction of the Reformation in the destruction of shrines and monasteries and the abolition of pilgrimages had the surprising result of popularising and interiorising the monastic concept of pilgrimage as never before. Pilgrimages had indeed become shockingly materialistic; they had to go; but the outward gear of pilgrimage provided the symbols of that inner devout life which led the new pilgrim to God. A poem popularly attributed to the Elizabethan courtier and pirate Raleigh was based on such imagery:

> Give me my scallop-shell of quiet,
> My staff of faith to walk upon,
> My scrip of joy, immortal diet,
> My bottle of salvation,
> My gown of glory, hope's true gage,
> And thus I'll take my pilgrimage.[30]

What now made a pilgrim was not the scrip, the gown, the staff, or the shell of St James, but travelling with Christ in a life-time of leaving self and receiving Him. Since the way into this new Jerusalem, the city of gold, had to be by a Cross and the river of death, the way of the pilgrim was not simple, light-hearted or easy. The image of journeying was to provide also the interior theme of the two great Catholic mystical writers of the sixteenth century; with Teresa of Avila, the pilgrimage was through the many mansions of a house, with

John of the Cross it was the ascent of a mountain where the way there is the way back and the way up is the way down and where you are is where you are not. It may well be that this inner concentration without outward expression placed too great a burden on the individual; but it was meant as a way of freedom and life.

I will conclude by quoting two pieces of literature from that world of earnest inner pilgrimage, which show I think that the essence of pilgrimage is an inescapable image always and everywhere. Since pilgrimage belongs to everyone, regardless of class or position, clerical or lay, monastic or secular, rich or poor, I have been happy to be able to chose these passages from two men whose positions were in the sharpest possible contrast. The first is by a bishop of Winchester, a courtier, the most learned man of his day, a friend of kings and princes; the second is by a poor brazier of Bedford who taught himself to read the Bible and who lay in prison when he wrote. The first is a section from one of Bishop Lancelot Andrewes' sermons on the Nativity, preached before James I at Whitehall on Christmas Day 1622 on the paradigm pilgrimage in Matthew 2:1-2, 'Behold, there came wise men from the east to Jerusalem.' The other, from the finest piece of all English pilgrimage literature, forms the conclusion of John Bunyan's *Pilgrim's Progress*, in which the pilgrimage of life finds its real end in death and the gateway to the Kingdom.

Andrewes began his sermon with his customary careful linguistic attention to the text, but concluded with an immediate application of the ideal for his hearers of coming to Christ, making the preliminary and to us surprising point that pilgrimage to Christ is not restricted to poor and ignorant shepherds:

Christ is not only for russet cloaks, shepherds and such, shews Himself to none but such. But even the grandees, great states such as these, *venerunt*, 'they came' too; and when they came were welcome to him. For they were sent for and invited by this star, their star properly.

He continued by summarising his account of the pilgrimage of the Magi (to us reminiscent of the use of this, and a subsequent sermon, by T.S. Eliot):

Whence? From the East, their own country. Whither? to Jerusalem ... They came a long journey ... . They came an uneasy journey ... And they came a dangerous journey ... And they came now, at the worst season of the year. And all but to do worship at Christ's birth. ... . So desirous were they to come with the first, and to be there as soon as possibly they might; broke through all these difficulties, *Et ecce venerunt*, 'And, behold, come they did.' ...

And these were wise men, and never a whit the less wise for so coming; nay never so truly wise in any thing they did, as in so coming.

The ideas of pilgrimage 'from' and 'towards' were both used here and were then given a new direction in which the inner pilgrimage was expressed in a new physical direction by an immediate application of the text to his hearers:

And how shall we that do? ....

And in the old Ritual of the Church we find that on the cover of the canister, wherein was the Sacrament of His body, there was a star engraven, to shew us that now the star leads us thither, to His body there.

And what shall I say now, but according as St John saith, and the star, and the wise men say, 'Come.' And He, Whose the star is, and to Whom the wise men came, saith 'Come.' And let them that are disposed, 'Come.' And let whosoever will, take of the 'Bread of Life which came down from Heaven' this day into Bethlehem, the house of bread. Of which Bread the Church is this day the house, the true

> Bethlehem, and all the Bethlehem we have now left to come
> to for the Bread of life, … . And this our nearest coming that
> here we can come, till we shall by another *venite* come, unto
> Him in His Heavenly Kingdom.[31]

This advice to make a pilgrimage to the altar, the house of bread, the new Bethlehem, showed a near and practical way through life for the Christian pilgrim; the inner pilgrimage could be helped by an outward ascent. There was a practical going in order to continue the inner one. But John Bunyan sounded a severer note in his account of the long pilgrimage of life made by Christian and his companions from the City of Destruction to the Valley of the Shadow of Death, through Vanity Fair, past the Slough of Despond, Giant Despair, and so to the Celestial City. As he guided Christian's wife, Christiana, on the way, Mr Valiant-for-Truth sang:

> Who would true Valour see
>   Let him come hither;
> One here will constant be,
>   Come wind, come weather;
> There's no Discouragement
>   Shall make him once relent,
> His first avow'd intent
>   To be a Pilgrim.[32]

Through all the difficulties of the way, the images of pilgrimage were meant to describe a pattern of inner progress in the Christian life—not a visible journey of any kind—but the story is so entrancing that it is easy to forget the stern reality conveyed. It is perhaps ironic that, while the problem with actual pilgrimage was the attraction of material excitements, in a similar way the difficulty with this account of inner pilgrimage is that its serious inner purpose can be nearly obscured by the pleasure of its imagery. A passage at the end expresses the new way of pilgrimage and makes clear that, under all the striking images, the pilgrim's progress had been as a *viator Christi*, as travelling through life with Christ:

> Then there came forth a summons for Mr. Stand-fast (this Mr. Stand-fast was he whom the pilgrims found upon his knees in the Enchanted Ground). When Mr. Stand-fast had thus set things in order, and the time being come for him to haste him away, he also went down to the river. Now there was a great calm at that time in the river; wherefore Mr. Stand-fast, when he was about half-way in, stood a while, and talked to his companions that had waited upon him thither.

This was not a river-crossing but a death, and Mr Stand-fast's reflections on his pilgrimage were concerned only with his life of conversion of heart, which he describes in a passage built up from biblical texts applied with personal relevance:

> And he said, 'This river has been a terror to many; yea, the thoughts of it have also frighted me; but now methinks I stand easy; I see myself now at the end of my journey; my toilsome days are ended. I am going to see that head which was crowned with thorns, and that face which was spit upon for me ... I have loved to hear my Lord spoken of; and wherever I have seen the print of His shoe in the earth, there I have coveted to set my foot too. His name has been to me as a civet-box; yea, sweeter than all perfumes. His voice to me has been most sweet, and His countenance I have more desired than they that have most desired the light of the sun. His Word I did use to gather for my food, and for antidotes against my faintings. He has held me, and hath kept me from mine iniquities; yea, my steps hath He strengthened in His way.'

For Andrewes and Bunyan the pilgrimage of the Christian was life itself, the end indeed death, and the way the way of the cross. 'Let us go forth therefore unto him without the camp bearing his reproach. For here we have no continuing city but we seek one to come.' (Hebrews 13:13, 14) That was the path of every Christian pilgrim, whether the way included actual walking or not. But however severe and demanding the life of pilgrimage might be, the end of the pilgrimage was delight, pleasure, wonder and love.

> Now while he was thus in discourse, his countenance changed, his strong man bowed under him; and, after he had said, 'Take me, for I come unto Thee!' he ceased to be seen of them.
>
> But glorious it was to see how the open region was filled with horses and chariots, with trumpeters and pipers, with singers and players on stringed instruments, to welcome the pilgrims as they went up, and followed one another in at the beautiful gate of the City. [33]

The path of a pilgrim has always had its pleasures and joys not only at the end but also in the experiences of shared love and delight on the way. After Christian had let go of his burden of sin at the wicket gate 'he gave three leaps for joy and went on his way singing'.[34] To recognise the seriousness of the undertaking of *peregrinatio* need not diminish the glory of the end, or prevent it from being reflected in the delights of the way itself. For any journey to be called a pilgrimage there has to be a serious element of going 'away from' and 'towards', but it means also a joyful sense of going out freely in good company with shared aim, which is, perhaps, to find that place which is most of all home:

> To an open house in the evening
> Home shall men come,
> To an older place than Eden
> And a taller town than Rome.
> To the end of the way of the wandering star,
> To the things that cannot be and that are,
> To the place where God was homeless
> And all men are at home.[35]

[1] George Herbert, 'Prayer', *Poems of George Herbert*, Oxford, 1961, p.44

[2] *Oxford Dictionary of the Christian Church*, ed. Cross and Livingstone, Oxford, 1997

[3] Geoffrey Chaucer, The Canterbury Tales, *Works of Geoffrey Chaucer*, ed. F. N. Robinson, Oxford, 1957, p.17

[4] William Langland, *Piers the Plowman*, trans. J.F. Goodridge, Harmondsworth, 1959, p.84

[5] I am indebted to Professor Peter Brown for the idea of the outsider/*peregrinus* especially in his seminal article 'The Rise and Function of the Holy Man in Late Antiquity', *Journal of Roman Studies* LX1 1971, pp.80-101

[6] Athanasius, *The Life of St Antony*, trans. Robert Mayer, London, 1950, pp.19-20

[7] *Sayings of the Desert Fathers: The Alphabetical Collection*, trans. Benedicta Ward, Oxford/Kalamazoo, 1975/84/98, Poemen 110, p.183

[8] *World of the Desert Fathers*, trans. Columba Stewart, Oxford 1975, vii (62), p.20

[9] *Anglo-Saxon Chronicle*, 891, ed. and trans. D Whitelock, in *English Historical Documents*, vol.1, c.500-1042, Oxford, 1979, pp.200-201

[10] *Felix's Life of St Guthlac of Crowland*, ed. and trans. Bertram Colgrave, Cambridge, 1956, xxv, p.88

[11] 'The Voyage of St Brendan', trans. J.F. Webb, in *The Age of Bede*, ed. David Farmer, Harmondsworth, 1965, p.213

[12] Palladius, *The Lausiac History*, trans. R.T. Meyer, London, 1965, no.37, Serapion, pp.108-9

[13] 'St Columba's Island Hermitage', *A Celtic Miscellany*, trans. K.Hurlston Jackson, Harmondsworth, 1951 p.223

[14] 'Wish of Manchan of Liath', ibid. p.223

[15] For a seminal discussion of this point, see R.W.Southern, *The Making of the Middle Ages*, London, 1953, chapter 5, From Epic to Romance, pp.209-245

[16] *The Principal Works of St Jerome*, Vol.VI, trans. W.F.Freemantle, W.B.Eerdmans, Michigan, 1979, Letter LVIII, To Paulinus, p.119

[17] ibid. Letter CXXV, To Rusticus, p.252

[18] ibid. Letter CVIII, To Eustochium, pp.195-224

[19] *The Pilgrimage of the Russian Abbot Daniel to the Holy Land*, trans. C.M.Wilson, London, 1888, p.405

[20] *Miracula S. Frideswidae*, by Prior Philip, *Acta Sanctorum*, Oct.8th no.10, pp.567-90

[21] *De Miraculis S. Mariae Laudunensis*, PL.156, cols.961-1020. (Also mentioned by Guibert of Nogent in his autobiography *De Vita Sua*)

[22] Chaucer op.cit. The Parson's Tale, p.229

[23] *Codex Calixtinus*, ed. Walter Muir Whitehill, Compostela, 1944, 2 Vols, Sermon *Veneranda Dies*, Vol. 2, p.144

[24] *Miracula S Anselmi* in *Memorials of St Anselm*, ed. R.W. Southern & F.C.Schmitt, *Auctores Britannici Medii Aevi* 1, London, 1969, pp.273-4

[25] ibid.

[26] Augustine, *City of God*, trans. H.Bettenson, Bk. XXII cap.30, p.1091

[27] Bede, *On the Temple*, trans. Sean Connolly, Liverpool, 1995, p.5

[28] Anselm, Proslogion cap. 22, trans. Benedicta Ward, *Prayers and Meditations of St Anselm with the Proslogion*, Harmondsworth, p.266

[29] *Letters of St Bernard of Clairvaux*, trans. Bruno Scott James, London, 1953, Letter 67, pp.90-92

[30] 'The Passionate Man's Pilgrimage' in *The Oxford Book of 16th Century Verse*, chosen by E.K. Chambers, Oxford, 1932, p.497

[31] Lancelot Andrewes, *Ninety-six Sermons*, Vol.1, Oxford 1841, pp.243-7

[32] John Bunyan, *Pilgrim's Progress*, London, 1890, p.365-366

[33] ibid. p.383

[34] ibid. p.59

[35] G.K.Chesterton, 'The House of Christmas', *Collected Poems of G.K.Chesterton*, London, 1933, p.140